The Reading Log

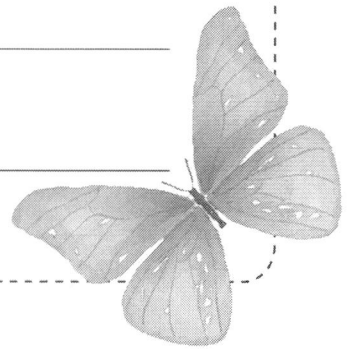

👤 _____

📞 _____

✉ _____

☰ _____

The Reading Log

Name : _____   Grade : _____

Academic Year : _____   Semester : _____

Date	Title Book	Min Read	Initials

The Reading Log

Name :

Grade :

Academic Year :

Semester :

Date	Title Book	Min Read	Initials

The Reading Log

Name : _____

Grade : _____

Academic Year : _____

Semester : _____

Date	Title Book	Min Read	Initials

The Reading Log

Name :

Grade :

Academic Year :

Semester :

Date	Title Book	Min Read	Initials

The Reading Log

Name : _____

Grade : _____

Academic Year : _____

Semester : _____

Date	Title Book	Min Read	Initials

The Reading Log

Name : _____

Grade : _____

Academic Year : _____

Semester : _____

Date	Title Book	Min Read	Initials

The Reading Log

Name : _____

Grade : _____

Academic Year : _____

Semester : _____

Date	Title Book	Min Read	Initials

The Reading Log

Name : _____

Grade : _____

Academic Year : _____

Semester : _____

Date	Title Book	Min Read	Initials

The Reading Log

Name : _____   Grade : _____

Academic Year : _____   Semester : _____

Date	Title Book	Min Read	Initials

The Reading Log

Name : _____   Grade : _____

Academic Year : _____   Semester : _____

Date	Title Book	Min Read	Initials

The Reading Log

Name : _____   Grade : _____

Academic Year : _____   Semester : _____

Date	Title Book	Min Read	Initials

The Reading Log

Name : _____

Grade : _____

Academic Year : _____

Semester : _____

Date	Title Book	Min Read	Initials

The Reading Log

Name : _____

Grade : _____

Academic Year : _____

Semester : _____

Date	Title Book	Min Read	Initials

The Reading Log

Name : _____   Grade : _____

Academic Year : _____   Semester : _____

Date	Title Book	Min Read	Initials

The Reading Log

Name : _____

Grade : _____

Academic Year : _____

Semester : _____

Date	Title Book	Min Read	Initials

The Reading Log

Name : _____

Grade : _____

Academic Year : _____

Semester : _____

Date	Title Book	Min Read	Initials

The Reading Log

Name : _____   Grade : _____

Academic Year : _____   Semester : _____

Date	Title Book	Min Read	Initials

The Reading Log

Name : _____

Grade : _____

Academic Year : _____

Semester : _____

Date	Title Book	Min Read	Initials

The Reading Log

Name : _____   Grade : _____

Academic Year : _____   Semester : _____

Date	Title Book	Min Read	Initials

The Reading Log

Name :

Grade :

Academic Year :

Semester :

Date	Title Book	Min Read	Initials

The Reading Log

Name : _____

Grade : _____

Academic Year : _____

Semester : _____

Date	Title Book	Min Read	Initials

The Reading Log

Name :

Grade :

Academic Year :

Semester :

Date	Title Book	Min Read	Initials

The Reading Log

Name :

Grade :

Academic Year :

Semester :

Date	Title Book	Min Read	Initials

The Reading Log

Name : _____

Grade : _____

Academic Year : _____

Semester : _____

Date	Title Book	Min Read	Initials

The Reading Log

Name : _____   Grade : _____

Academic Year : _____   Semester : _____

Date	Title Book	Min Read	Initials

The Reading Log

Name : _____

Grade : _____

Academic Year : _____

Semester : _____

Date	Title Book	Min Read	Initials

The Reading Log

Name : _____

Grade : _____

Academic Year : _____

Semester : _____

Date	Title Book	Min Read	Initials

The Reading Log

Name : _____

Grade : _____

Academic Year : _____

Semester : _____

Date	Title Book	Min Read	Initials

The Reading Log

Name : _____

Grade : _____

Academic Year : _____

Semester : _____

Date	Title Book	Min Read	Initials

The Reading Log

Name : _____

Grade : _____

Academic Year : _____

Semester : _____

Date	Title Book	Min Read	Initials

The Reading Log

Name : _____

Grade : _____

Academic Year : _____

Semester : _____

Date	Title Book	Min Read	Initials

The Reading Log

Name : _____   Grade : _____

Academic Year : _____   Semester : _____

Date	Title Book	Min Read	Initials

The Reading Log

Name : _____   Grade : _____

Academic Year : _____   Semester : _____

Date	Title Book	Min Read	Initials

The Reading Log

Name : _____   Grade : _____

Academic Year : _____   Semester : _____

Date	Title Book	Min Read	Initials

The Reading Log

Name : _____   Grade : _____

Academic Year : _____   Semester : _____

Date	Title Book	Min Read	Initials

The Reading Log

Name : _____   Grade : _____

Academic Year : _____   Semester : _____

Date	Title Book	Min Read	Initials

The Reading Log

Name : _____   Grade : _____

Academic Year : _____   Semester : _____

Date	Title Book	Min Read	Initials

The Reading Log

Name : _____   Grade : _____

Academic Year : _____   Semester : _____

Date	Title Book	Min Read	Initials

The Reading Log

Name : _____

Grade : _____

Academic Year : _____

Semester : _____

Date	Title Book	Min Read	Initials

The Reading Log

Name : _____

Grade : _____

Academic Year : _____

Semester : _____

Date	Title Book	Min Read	Initials

The Reading Log

Name : _____

Grade : _____

Academic Year : _____

Semester : _____

Date	Title Book	Min Read	Initials

The Reading Log

Name :

Grade :

Academic Year :

Semester :

Date	Title Book	Min Read	Initials

The Reading Log

Name : _____   Grade : _____

Academic Year : _____   Semester : _____

Date	Title Book	Min Read	Initials

The Reading Log

Name :

Grade :

Academic Year :

Semester :

Date	Title Book	Min Read	Initials

The Reading Log

Name : _____   Grade : _____

Academic Year : _____   Semester : _____

Date	Title Book	Min Read	Initials

The Reading Log

Name : _____   Grade : _____

Academic Year : _____   Semester : _____

Date	Title Book	Min Read	Initials

The Reading Log

Name : _____

Grade : _____

Academic Year : _____

Semester : _____

Date	Title Book	Min Read	Initials

The Reading Log

Name :

Grade :

Academic Year :

Semester :

Date	Title Book	Min Read	Initials

The Reading Log

Name : _____

Grade : _____

Academic Year : _____

Semester : _____

Date	Title Book	Min Read	Initials

The Reading Log

Name : _____

Grade : _____

Academic Year : _____

Semester : _____

Date	Title Book	Min Read	Initials

The Reading Log

Name : _____   Grade : _____

Academic Year : _____   Semester : _____

Date	Title Book	Min Read	Initials

The Reading Log

Name : _____

Grade : _____

Academic Year : _____

Semester : _____

Date	Title Book	Min Read	Initials

The Reading Log

Name : _____

Grade : _____

Academic Year : _____

Semester : _____

Date	Title Book	Min Read	Initials

The Reading Log

Name :

Grade :

Academic Year :

Semester :

Date	Title Book	Min Read	Initials

The Reading Log

Name : _____

Grade : _____

Academic Year : _____

Semester : _____

Date	Title Book	Min Read	Initials

The Reading Log

Name : _____

Grade : _____

Academic Year : _____

Semester : _____

Date	Title Book	Min Read	Initials

The Reading Log

Name : _____

Grade : _____

Academic Year : _____

Semester : _____

Date	Title Book	Min Read	Initials

The Reading Log

Name :

Grade :

Academic Year :

Semester :

Date	Title Book	Min Read	Initials

The Reading Log

Name : _____   Grade : _____

Academic Year : _____   Semester : _____

Date	Title Book	Min Read	Initials

The Reading Log

Name :

Grade :

Academic Year :

Semester :

Date	Title Book	Min Read	Initials

The Reading Log

Name : _____

Grade : _____

Academic Year : _____

Semester : _____

Date	Title Book	Min Read	Initials

The Reading Log

Name :

Grade :

Academic Year :

Semester :

Date	Title Book	Min Read	Initials

The Reading Log

Name : _____

Grade : _____

Academic Year : _____

Semester : _____

Date	Title Book	Min Read	Initials

The Reading Log

Name : _____

Grade : _____

Academic Year : _____

Semester : _____

Date	Title Book	Min Read	Initials

The Reading Log

Name : _____   Grade : _____

Academic Year : _____   Semester : _____

Date	Title Book	Min Read	Initials

The Reading Log

Name :

Grade :

Academic Year :

Semester :

Date	Title Book	Min Read	Initials

The Reading Log

Name : _____

Grade : _____

Academic Year : _____

Semester : _____

Date	Title Book	Min Read	Initials

The Reading Log

Name : _____

Grade : _____

Academic Year : _____

Semester : _____

Date	Title Book	Min Read	Initials

The Reading Log

Name : _____   Grade : _____

Academic Year : _____   Semester : _____

Date	Title Book	Min Read	Initials

The Reading Log

Name : _____

Grade : _____

Academic Year : _____

Semester : _____

Date	Title Book	Min Read	Initials

The Reading Log

Name :

Grade :

Academic Year :

Semester :

Date	Title Book	Min Read	Initials

The Reading Log

Name : _____

Grade : _____

Academic Year : _____

Semester : _____

Date	Title Book	Min Read	Initials

The Reading Log

Name : _____   Grade : _____

Academic Year : _____   Semester : _____

Date	Title Book	Min Read	Initials

The Reading Log

Name :

Grade :

Academic Year :

Semester :

Date	Title Book	Min Read	Initials

The Reading Log

Name : _____

Grade : _____

Academic Year : _____

Semester : _____

Date	Title Book	Min Read	Initials

The Reading Log

Name : _____   Grade : _____

Academic Year : _____   Semester : _____

Date	Title Book	Min Read	Initials

The Reading Log

Name : _____

Grade : _____

Academic Year : _____

Semester : _____

Date	Title Book	Min Read	Initials

The Reading Log

Name : _____   Grade : _____

Academic Year : _____   Semester : _____

Date	Title Book	Min Read	Initials

The Reading Log

Name :

Grade :

Academic Year :

Semester :

Date	Title Book	Min Read	Initials

The Reading Log

Name :

Grade :

Academic Year :

Semester :

Date	Title Book	Min Read	Initials

The Reading Log

Name : _____   Grade : _____

Academic Year : _____   Semester : _____

Date	Title Book	Min Read	Initials

The Reading Log

Name : _____   Grade : _____

Academic Year : _____   Semester : _____

Date	Title Book	Min Read	Initials

The Reading Log

Name : _____

Grade : _____

Academic Year : _____

Semester : _____

Date	Title Book	Min Read	Initials

The Reading Log

Name : _____

Grade : _____

Academic Year : _____

Semester : _____

Date	Title Book	Min Read	Initials

The Reading Log

Name : _____   Grade : _____

Academic Year : _____   Semester : _____

Date	Title Book	Min Read	Initials

The Reading Log

Name :

Grade :

Academic Year :

Semester :

Date	Title Book	Min Read	Initials

The Reading Log

Name : _____

Grade : _____

Academic Year : _____

Semester : _____

Date	Title Book	Min Read	Initials

The Reading Log

Name : _____

Grade : _____

Academic Year : _____

Semester : _____

Date	Title Book	Min Read	Initials

The Reading Log

Name : _____   Grade : _____

Academic Year : _____   Semester : _____

Date	Title Book	Min Read	Initials

The Reading Log

Name :

Grade :

Academic Year :

Semester :

Date	Title Book	Min Read	Initials

The Reading Log

Name : _____

Grade : _____

Academic Year : _____

Semester : _____

Date	Title Book	Min Read	Initials

The Reading Log

Name : _____

Grade : _____

Academic Year : _____

Semester : _____

Date	Title Book	Min Read	Initials

The Reading Log

Name :

Grade :

Academic Year :

Semester :

Date	Title Book	Min Read	Initials

The Reading Log

Name : _____

Grade : _____

Academic Year : _____

Semester : _____

Date	Title Book	Min Read	Initials

The Reading Log

Name : _____

Grade : _____

Academic Year : _____

Semester : _____

Date	Title Book	Min Read	Initials

The Reading Log

Name :

Grade :

Academic Year :

Semester :

Date	Title Book	Min Read	Initials

The Reading Log

Name : _____   Grade : _____

Academic Year : _____   Semester : _____

Date	Title Book	Min Read	Initials

The Reading Log

Name :

Grade :

Academic Year :

Semester :

Date	Title Book	Min Read	Initials

The Reading Log

Name : _____   Grade : _____

Academic Year : _____   Semester : _____

Date	Title Book	Min Read	Initials

Made in the USA
Columbia, SC
03 July 2023